שערי סליחה

Gates of Forgiveness

אל ארך אפים אתה, ובעל הרחמים נקראת, ודרך תשובה
הורית.

You are a God whose patience is endless; You are called
Supreme in Mercy, and You show us the way to turn.

– Selichot

ויאמר יי: סלחתי כדברך.

And the Lord said: I have pardoned in response to your plea.

– Numbers 15.19

שערי סליחה

GATES OF
FORGIVENESS

The Union Selichot Service

*A Service of Preparation
for the
Days of Awe*

CENTRAL CONFERENCE OF AMERICAN RABBIS
5740 New York 1980

ISBN 0-916694-57-7
PRINTED IN U.S.A.

Contents

Introduction

"I will give you a new heart; a new spirit will I place within you." With this divine promise the Torah captures the essence of the experience of repentance and atonement, an experience that begins with self-examination and confession, and reaches its climax in pardon and renewal.

Our prayers for forgiveness are called Selichot, penitential prayers. Originally recited on Fast Days (instituted to avert or to mourn disasters) and then on Yom Kippur, the recitation of Selichot came to be extended, in time, to Rosh Hashanah and the Ten Days of Repentance. The Sefardim recite Selichot from the first of Elul, the month preceding Rosh Hashanah, while the Ashkenazim recite Selichot from the Sunday before Rosh Hashanah (midnight Saturday night) or, when Rosh Hashanah falls on a Monday or Tuesday, from two Sundays before Rosh Hashanah.

These prayers are a preparation for the penitential season. Thus their subject-matter includes reflections on human life and on divine mercy, petitions for relief from suffering and persecution, confessions of sin and pleas for forgiveness. In Reform Judaism, the practice of reciting Selichot before Rosh Hashanah faded for a time. Of late, however, interest has revived. Many Selichot liturgies have been prepared by individual Reform rabbis. But this is the first liturgy to be published by the Central Conference of American Rabbis. Its publication alongside *Shaarei Teshuvah, Gates of Repentance* completes our new liturgy for the Days of Awe.

A few words now about this service. It draws upon the traditional prayers of Selichot, but is in the main a new creation, with a number of striking innovations. Since Selichot is recited on Saturday night, we begin with Havdalah, the service that separates Shabbat from the weekdays, the holy from the profane. A series of Meditations and Readings on themes appropriate to the occasion is then provided. These come from classic and contemporary Jewish sources. Selichot itself is understood by us as the service in which the House of Israel, individually and collectively, struggles to return to God as we prepare for the Days of Awe. For that reason, our service follows a clearly delineated pattern. We begin with a call to return. That call raises the question: Who is called, and what is the nature of the people that hears the call and attempts to make its response? So the second section of the service speaks of and to the House of Israel, the people called by God again and again to return. But to whom or what do we turn? Our third section, then, concerns the God to whom we turn, and the nature—so far as we can describe it—of the relationship between Israel as God's people and the Holy One as Israel's God. Having come this far, we are able to confront God in a different way. Sinners ourselves, and ready to acknowledge it, we invoke the divine compassion as a prelude to our acknowledgment of sin. Confession made, we conclude with a fervent turning to God before the open Ark, symbol of God's presence in our midst. Throughout the service, we utilize themes and passages that are found in the services for the Days of Awe, so that the service becomes rather like an overture to an opera, where themes are introduced that will be developed more fully later, especially on Yom Kippur. We have made use of our classical heritage of penitential literature for this purpose, but most of the readings, prayers, and meditations in this service are contemporary. Together may the old and the new help us to find a new heart and a new spirit.

לֵב טָהוֹר בְּרָא־לִי, אֱלֹהִים, וְרוּחַ נָכוֹן חַדֵּשׁ בְּקִרְבִּי.

ערב שבת קדש 'וארא' תש"ם

29 Tevet 5740

Chaim Stern,
CHAPPAQUA, NEW YORK

A Note on Usage

As in the earlier volumes of this series (*Gates of Prayer, Gates of the House,* and *Gates of Repentance*) the typeface suggests how the service might be conducted. In place of the conventional rubrics 'Reader,' 'All Reading,' 'Singing,' and the like, we use Roman type for 'Reader,' *italics* for 'All Reading,' and smaller Roman type (in the English) for Hebrew passages that are generally sung. In congregations where a Cantor shares the service, some of the 'Reader' passages will no doubt be chanted.

The prayerbook is divided into three sections. Since the service is held on Saturday night, we begin with Havdalah. The Meditations and Readings following are arranged thematically and may be read consecutively, if desired. This section, or selections from it, might be read silently or aloud, either before or during the Selichot service, which it precedes. It might also be the basis of exposition and discussion preceding Selichot. Finally, the Selichot service itself follows the Meditations and Readings, and we conclude this volume with Notes for those who wish to know the sources of the material contained in it.

This prayerbook affords each congregation latitude in establishing its own patterns of worship. Local custom or necessity will prescribe what will be read and what sung, what in Hebrew and what in English, what will be set for silent meditation and what will be spoken. While Hebrew and English are generally set on the same page, it is not contemplated that all Hebrew and English passages will be read in the course of a single service.

הבדלה

HAVDALAH

HAVDALAH

The candle is lit

הִנֵּה אֵל יְשׁוּעָתִי, אֶבְטַח וְלֹא אֶפְחָד.

כִּי עָזִּי וְזִמְרָת יָהּ יְיָ, וַיְהִי־לִי לִישׁוּעָה.

וּשְׁאַבְתֶּם מַיִם בְּשָׂשׂוֹן מִמַּעַיְנֵי הַיְשׁוּעָה.

לַיְיָ הַיְשׁוּעָה, עַל־עַמְּךָ בִרְכָתֶךָ, סֶּלָה.

יְיָ צְבָאוֹת עִמָּנוּ, מִשְׂגַּב־לָנוּ אֱלֹהֵי יַעֲקֹב, סֶלָה.

יְיָ צְבָאוֹת, אַשְׁרֵי אָדָם בֹּטֵחַ בָּךְ!

Behold, God is my Deliverer; trusting in the Lord, I am not afraid.

For the Lord is my Strength and my Stronghold, the Source of my deliverance.

With joy shall we draw water from the wells of salvation.

The Lord brings deliverance, and blessing to the people.

The Lord of Hosts is with us; the God of Jacob is our stronghold.

O Lord of all the universe, happy is the one who trusts in You!

יְיָ, הוֹשִׁיעָה; הַמֶּלֶךְ יַעֲנֵנוּ בְיוֹם־קָרְאֵנוּ.

לַיְהוּדִים הָיְתָה אוֹרָה וְשִׂמְחָה, וְשָׂשׂוֹן וִיקָר; כֵּן תִּהְיֶה לָנוּ.

כּוֹס יְשׁוּעוֹת אֶשָּׂא, וּבְשֵׁם יְיָ אֶקְרָא.

Save us, O Lord; answer us, O King, when we call upon You. Give us light and joy, gladness and honor, as in the happiest days of Israel's past.

Then we will lift up the cup to rejoice in Your saving power, and call out Your name in praise.

◇◇

The cup of wine is raised

בָּרוּךְ אַתָּה, יְיָ אֱלֹהֵינוּ, מֶלֶךְ הָעוֹלָם, בּוֹרֵא פְּרִי הַגָּפֶן.

Blessed is the Lord our God, Ruler of the universe, Creator of the fruit of the vine.

The spice-box is held up

בָּרוּךְ אַתָּה, יְיָ אֱלֹהֵינוּ, מֶלֶךְ הָעוֹלָם, בּוֹרֵא מִינֵי בְשָׂמִים.

Blessed is the Lord our God, Ruler of the universe, Creator of all the spices.

The candle is held up

בָּרוּךְ אַתָּה, יְיָ אֱלֹהֵינוּ, מֶלֶךְ הָעוֹלָם, בּוֹרֵא מְאוֹרֵי הָאֵשׁ.

Blessed is the Lord our God, Ruler of the universe, Creator of the light of fire.

◇

בָּרוּךְ אַתָּה, יְיָ אֱלֹהֵינוּ, מֶלֶךְ הָעוֹלָם, הַמַּבְדִּיל בֵּין קֹדֶשׁ לְחוֹל, בֵּין אוֹר לְחְשֶׁךְ, בֵּין יִשְׂרָאֵל לָעַמִּים, בֵּין

4

יוֹם הַשְּׁבִיעִי לְשֵׁשֶׁת יְמֵי הַמַּעֲשֶׂה. בָּרוּךְ אַתָּה, יְיָ,
הַמַּבְדִּיל בֵּין קֹדֶשׁ לְחוֹל.

Blessed is the Lord our God, Ruler of the universe, who
separates sacred from profane, light from darkness, the
House of Israel from other peoples, and the seventh day of
rest from the six days of labor.

Blessed is the Lord, who separates the sacred from the profane.

The candle is extinguished

◇◇

Elijah!
Week after week we wait,
at Sabbath's end we wait for you,
we wait to be redeemed:
from guilt and oppression redeemed;

from lonely days redeemed;

from empty nights redeemed;

and from the stuttering of our hearts,
from that, too, redeemed.

Do you wait for us?
Do you await one sign,
one deed, one surprise?

Yes, yes! You wait for us,
you wait for us to wait no more.

Help us. Help us turn.
Help us turn, to begin to turn.

5

Ei·li·ya·hu ha·na·vi,   אֵלִיָּהוּ הַנָּבִיא,

Ei·li·ya·hu ha·tish·bi;   אֵלִיָּהוּ הַתִּשְׁבִּי;

Ei·li·ya·hu, Ei·li·ya·hu,   אֵלִיָּהוּ, אֵלִיָּהוּ,

Ei·li·ya·hu ha·gil·a·di.   אֵלִיָּהוּ הַגִּלְעָדִי.

Bi·me·hei·ra ve·ya·mei·nu,   בִּמְהֵרָה בְיָמֵינוּ,

ya·vo ei·lei·nu;   יָבֹא אֵלֵינוּ;

im ma·shi·ach ben Da·vid,   עִם מָשִׁיחַ בֶּן דָּוִד,

im ma·shi·ach ben Da·vid.   עִם מָשִׁיחַ בֶּן דָּוִד.

Ei·li·ya·hu . . .   . . . אֵלִיָּהוּ

◇◇

Ha·mav·dil bein ko·desh le·chol,   הַמַּבְדִּיל בֵּין קֹדֶשׁ לְחוֹל,

cha·to·tei·nu hu yim·chol,   חַטֹּאתֵנוּ הוּא יִמְחֹל,

zar·ei·nu ve·chas·pei·nu   זַרְעֵנוּ וְכַסְפֵּנוּ

    yar·beh ka·chol,   יַרְבֶּה כַּחוֹל,

ve·cha·ko·cha·vim ba·lai·la.   וְכַכּוֹכָבִים בַּלָּיְלָה.

Sha·vu·a tov . . .   . . . שָׁבוּעַ טוֹב

Yom pa·na ke·tseil to·mer,   יוֹם פָּנָה כְּצֵל תֹּמֶר,

Ek·ra la·eil, a·lai go·meir;   אֶקְרָא לָאֵל, עָלַי גֹּמֵר;

a·mar sho·meir, a·ta vo·ker,   אָמַר שׁוֹמֵר, אָתָא בֹקֶר,

ve·gam lai·la.   וְגַם־לָיְלָה.

Sha·vu·a tov . . .   . . . שָׁבוּעַ טוֹב

Tsid·ka·te·cha ke·har Ta·vor,	צִדְקָתְךָ כְּהַר תָּבוֹר,
al cha·ta·ai a·vor ta·a·vor,	עַל חֲטָאַי עָבוֹר תַּעֲבוֹר,
ke·yom et·mol ki ya·a·vor,	כְּיוֹם אֶתְמוֹל כִּי יַעֲבוֹר,
ve·ash·mu·ra va·lai·la.	וְאַשְׁמוּרָה בַלָּיְלָה.
Sha·vu·a tov . . .	שָׁבוּעַ טוֹב . . .

Hei·a·teir, no·ra ve·a·yom,	הֶעָתֵר, נוֹרָא וְאָיוֹם,
a·sha·vei·a, te·na fid·yom,	אֲשַׁוֵּעַ, תְּנָה פִדְיוֹם,
be·ne·shef, be·e·rev yom,	בְּנֶשֶׁף, בְּעֶרֶב יוֹם,
be·i·shon lai·la.	בְּאִישׁוֹן לָיְלָה.
Sha·vu·a tov . . .	שָׁבוּעַ טוֹב . . .

You separate sacred from profane: separate us now from our sins! Let those who love You be as many as the sands, and as the stars of heaven.

Day has declined, the shadows are gone; we call to the One whose word is good. The sentry says: 'Morning will come, though it still be night.'

Your righteousness is a majestic mountain; forgive our sins. Let them be as yesterday when it is past, as a watch in the night.

Hear our prayer, O awesome God, and grant redemption! In the twilight, in the waning of the day, or in the blackness of the night!

הגיונות

MEDITATIONS AND READINGS

1

God does not want to be believed in, to be debated and defended by us, but simply to be realized through us.

2

Religion is essentially the act of holding fast to God. And that does not mean holding fast to an image that one has made of God, nor even holding fast to the faith in God that one has conceived. It means holding fast to the existing God. The earth would not hold fast to its conception of the sun (if it had one) nor to its connection with it, but to the sun itself.

3

It is not necessary to know something of God in order really to believe in God; many true believers know how to talk to God but not about God.

4

We can speak only in metaphor of the eternal and infinite. If we wish to describe the indescribable, we can do so only by poetry. All endeavors to reach God by words resolve themselves into religious poetry. When we experience the hidden, the unfathomable, we can respond with the devoutness of silence . . . or with poetry and prayer we can sing of the ineffable.

5

The best worship of God is silence and hope.

6

"I am prayer (Psalm 109.4)." There are three rungs to this ladder. Third best is to talk about prayer. Second best is to pray. Best is to *be* prayer.

7

The Jews have always been a minority. But a minority is compelled to think; that is the blessing of its fate. The conviction of the few is expressed through the energy of constant searching and finding.

8

The Jew is the great nonconformist, the great dissenter of history. That is the purpose of our existence. That is why our fight for religion has had to be a fight for self-preservation. In this fight there is no thought of might, but rather of individuality and personality for the sake of the eternal—not might but strength.

9

It requires religious courage to belong to a minority such as Judaism always has been and always will be; for many days will come and go before the messianic time arrives. It requires ethical courage to be a Jew when all worldly comforts, honors and prizes lure us to the other side.

10

Jewish history, in its tragedy and dignity, is a history of choice, a resolve on behalf of God, and therefore a history full of suffering. The Jewish people never became the mere object of its fate; it remained a creator, full of resolve and upright in spirit even in times of affliction. In a history which merely recounts external events, the Jews seem to be tossed about as a plaything of nations. But in a history which looks to spiritual power and activity, the Jewish people is seen as a force making its own decisions and effecting its genuine realization: its life is a fulfillment. Its history possesses nobility, if true nobility is taken to mean a unity of inheritance and achievement; it possesses faith and deed, growth and accomplishment. This nobility Judaism assigns to each individual.

11

The Torah was not given to angels.
The Torah speaks in the language of human beings.

12

Is there a truth we can possess? Can we appropriate it? There certainly is none we can pick up and put in our pocket. But the individual can have an honest and un-compromising relationship to truth and hold and uphold it always. Human truth becomes real when one tries to translate one's relationship to truth into the reality of one's life. One does not reflect upon it, one does not express it, one does not perceive it, but one lives it and receives it as life.

13

Our life is fulfilled by what we become, not by what we were at birth. Endowment and heritage mean much . . . and then again nothing; the essential thing is what we make of them.

14

Whoever bears the human visage was created and called to be a revelation of human dignity.

15

If you wish to fulfill the commandment to judge your neighbor with justice, then judge every human being for the best.

16

The kingdom of God is built by working for our neighbor.

17

Every ethical deed and every decision for the good is a sanctification of God's name; such deeds and decisions are a realization of the divine, and through them is established a sanctuary of the good upon earth, a place prepared for the kingdom of God.

18

One does not serve God with the spirit only, but with the whole of one's nature, without any subtractions. There is not one realm of the spirit and another of nature; there is only the growing kingdom of God.

19

If you divide your life between God and the world, through giving the world 'what is its' to save for God 'what is God's,' you are denying God the service the Holy One demands: to hallow the everyday in the world and the soul.

20

They are most lonely who love only themselves.

21

To love somebody is not just a strong feeling—it is a decision, it is a judgment, it is a promise. If love were only a feeling there would be no basis for the promise to love each other for ever. A feeling comes and it may go. How can I judge that it will stay for ever, when my act does not involve judgment and decision?

22

Of all qualities, sadness is the worst. It is the attribute of the incurable egotist, who is always thinking: 'This should have been mine; I have been wrongfully deprived of that.' It is always *I*.

23

You may give liberally, and yet because you give unlovingly and wound the heart of the poor, your gift is in vain, for it has lost the attribute of charity. You may give little, but because your heart goes with it, your deed is blessed and you are blessed.

24

The most beautiful thing that one can do is to forgive a wrong.

25

Days are scrolls; write on them what you want to be remembered.

26

You cannot say to the Angel of Death: I wish to arrange my affairs before I die.

27

I am afraid of things that cannot harm me, and I know it. I yearn for things that cannot help me, and I know it. What I fear is within me, and within me, too, is what I seek.

28

Existence will remain meaningless for you if you yourself do not penetrate into it with active love and if you do not in this way discover its meaning for yourself.
If you wish to believe, love! One who loves brings God and the world together.

29

Only an existence that is not content with the mere fact of existence can have any value.

30

Only when atonement is not limited to a mere personal consciousness of salvation does it carry within itself the new ethical impulse that leads to a deepening of morality. In atonement's purification, our conscience becomes more profoundly alive. Atonement brings ethical strength. In profound contrast to the idea of redemption as a goal of rest stands the Jewish idea of redemption as a continuous ethical ascent.

31

The men and women in the Bible are sinners like ourselves, but there is one sin they do not commit, our arch-sin: they do not dare confine God to a circumscribed space or division of life, 'religion.' They have not the insolence to draw boundaries around God's commandments and say: 'Up to this point you are sovereign, but beyond these bounds begins the sovereignty of science or society or the state.'

32

The older we get, the greater becomes our inclination to give thanks, especially heavenwards. We feel more strongly than we could possibly have felt before that life is a free gift, and receive every unqualifiedly good hour in gratefully reaching out hands, as an unexpected gift.

But we also feel, again and again, an urge to thank our brothers and sisters, even if they have not done anything special for us. For what, then? For really meeting me when we met; for opening your eyes, and not mistaking me for someone else; for opening your ears, and listening carefully to what I had to say to you; indeed, for opening up to me what I really want to address—your securely locked heart.

33

We know nothing about death, nothing beyond the one fact that we shall 'die'—but what is that, to die? We do not know. We must therefore assume that death constitutes the final limit of all that we are able to imagine. The desire to extend our imagination into the beyond of dying, to anticipate psychically what death alone can reveal to us existentially, seems to me a lack of faith disguised as faith. Genuine faith says: I know nothing about death, but I do know that God is eternity; and I also know that God is my God.

סליחות

SELICHOT

בְּמוֹצָאֵי מְנוּחָה, קִדַּמְנוּךְ תְּחִלָּה.
הַט אָזְנְךָ מִמָּרוֹם, יוֹשֵׁב תְּהִלָּה,
לִשְׁמֹעַ אֶל הָרִנָּה וְאֶל הַתְּפִלָּה.

Shabbat has ended; still we stand before You.
O God of praises, hearken from on high.
O hear our song and our prayer.

אֶת־יְמִין עֹז עוֹרְרָה לַעֲשׂוֹת חָיִל
בְּצֶדֶק נֶעֱקַד, וְנִשְׁחַט תְּמוּרוֹ אָיִל.
גְּנָן נָא גִזְעוֹ בְּזַעֲקָם בְּעוֹד לָיִל,
לִשְׁמֹעַ אֶל הָרִנָּה וְאֶל הַתְּפִלָּה.

For Father Isaac's sake, who gave himself to You,
Shield his children who cry to You this night.
O hear our song and our prayer.

דְּרָשׁ נָא דוֹרְשֶׁיךָ בְּדָרְשָׁם פָּנֶיךָ,
הִדָּרֶשׁ לָמוֹ מִשְּׁמֵי מְעוֹנֶךָ,
וּלְשַׁוְעַת חִנּוּנָם אַל תַּעְלֵם אָזְנֶךָ
לִשְׁמֹעַ אֶל הָרִנָּה וְאֶל הַתְּפִלָּה.

From heaven's heights turn to us who turn to You,
To all who in singleness of heart seek You.
O hear our song and our prayer.

זוֹחֲלִים וְרוֹעֲדִים מִיּוֹם בּוֹאֶךָ,
חָלִים כְּמַבְכִּירָה מֵעֶבְרַת מַשָּׂאֶךָ,

טְנוּפָם מְחֵה נָא וְיוֹדוּ פְּלָאֶיךָ
לִשְׁמֹעַ אֶל הָרִנָּה וְאֶל הַתְּפִלָּה.

Trembling in Your presence like a woman in travail,
Humbly we beseech: Blot out our transgressions.
O hear our song and our prayer.

יוֹצֵר אַתָּה לְכָל־יְצִיר נוֹצָר.
כּוֹנַנְתָּ מֵאָז תֶּרֶף לְחַלְצָם מִמַּעֲצָר
לְחָנְנָם חִנָּם מֵאוֹצָר הַמְנֻצָּר,
לִשְׁמֹעַ אֶל הָרִנָּה וְאֶל הַתְּפִלָּה.

Creator of Your world's every creature,
Sustainer of all, sustain us now.
O hear our song and our prayer.

מָרוֹם אִם עָצְמוּ פִּשְׁעֵי קְהָלֶךָ,
נָא שַׂגְּבֵם מֵאוֹצָר הַמּוּכָן בִּזְבוּלֶךָ,
עָדֶיךָ לָחֹן חִנָּם בָּאִים אֵלֶיךָ
לִשְׁמֹעַ אֶל הָרִנָּה וְאֶל הַתְּפִלָּה.

Though the sins of Your people are too many to count,
We plead for Your mercy, Exalted One. Raise us up once
more.
O hear our song and our prayer.

פְּנֵה נָא אֶל הַתְּלָאוֹת וְאַל לְחַטָּאוֹת,
צַדֵּק צוֹעֲקֶיךָ, מַפְלִיא פְּלָאוֹת,
קְשָׁב נָא חִנוּנָם, אֱלֹהִים יְיָ צְבָאוֹת,
לִשְׁמֹעַ אֶל הָרִנָּה וְאֶל הַתְּפִלָּה.

Have regard to our suffering and not to our shortcomings,
Cleanse us who cry out to You, Wondrous God.
O hear our song and our prayer.

רְצֵה עֲתִירָתָם בְּעָמְדָם בַּלֵּילוֹת,
שְׁעֵה בְּרָצוֹן כְּקָרְבַּן כָּלִיל וְעוֹלוֹת,
תַּרְאֵם נִסֶּיךָ, עוֹשֶׂה גְדוֹלוֹת,
לִשְׁמְעַ אֶל הָרִנָּה וְאֶל הַתְּפִלָּה.

Be our offering this night acceptable as sacrifice of old.
Maker of miracles, make us to see the miracle of forgive-
ness.
O hear our song and our prayer.

◇◇

TURNING: THE CALL

Now is the time for turning. The leaves are beginning to
turn from green to red and orange. The birds are beginning to turn and are heading once more toward the South.
The animals are beginning to turn to storing their food for
the winter. For leaves, birds, and animals turning comes
instinctively. But for us turning does not come so easily. It
takes an act of will for us to make a turn. It means break-
ing with old habits. It means admitting that we have been
wrong; and this is never easy. It means losing face; it
means starting all over again; and this is always painful. It
means saying: I am sorry. It means recognizing that we
have the ability to change. These things are terribly hard
to do. But unless we turn, we will be trapped forever in
yesterday's ways. Lord, help us to turn—from callousness

23

to sensitivity, from hostility to love, from pettiness to purpose, from envy to contentment, from carelessness to discipline, from fear to faith. Turn us around, O Lord, and bring us back toward You. Revive our lives, as at the beginning. And turn us toward each other, Lord, for in isolation there is no life.

◇

Ha·shi·vei·nu A·do·nai ei·le·cha,

ve·na·shu·vah.

cha·deish ya·mei·nu ke·ke·dem.

הֲשִׁיבֵנוּ יְיָ אֵלֶיךָ,

וְנָשׁוּבָה.

חַדֵּשׁ יָמֵינוּ כְּקֶדֶם.

Help us to return to You, O Lord; then truly shall we return.
Renew our days as in the past.

◇

Eternal God, what can we say in Your presence? How account for our sins? We speak of repentance, and yet are slow to change. But now we turn to You with the prayer that Your love may abide with us always, turning our hearts to Your ways, our feet to Your paths. Hope is food and drink to us; hope sustains us. And so we pray: Do not turn us away empty-handed from Your presence. End our darkness with Your light and turn our passions to Your purpose. Help us, Lord, in this hour of turning, to make real in our lives the words of our mouths, the meditations of our hearts.

MEDITATION

I have been one acquainted with the night.
I have walked out in rain—and back in rain.
I have outwalked the furthest city light.

I have looked down the saddest lane.
I have passed by the watchman on his beat
And dropped my eyes, unwilling to explain.

I have stood still and stopped the sound of feet
When far away an interrupted cry
Came over houses from another street,

But not to call me back or say goodbye;
And further still at an unearthly height,
One luminary clock against the sky

Proclaimed the time was neither wrong nor right.
I have been one acquainted with the night.

◇◇

Return, O Israel, to the Lord your God;
return, all you who have stumbled.
For thus says the Eternal God,
the Holy One of Israel:
In returning, in peace, shall you triumph;
in calm trust you shall find strength.

You are a stronghold to the poor,
a shelter from the storm,
a shade from the heat.

Lord, let me return to You,
let me come to You,

25

reach out to me,
I am alone.
Alone.
Empty-hearted.
Afraid of myself.
Let me come to You.
Reach out to me.

You are a shelter from the storm,
a shade from the heat.

Return, O Israel, to the Lord your God.
Behold how the Eternal One does great things
with this people!
Behold the Most High,
who heaps miracle upon wonder!
Return, O Israel, return!

You are a stronghold to the poor,
a crown of glory to all who stumble and fall,
to all who rise and return!

◇◇

Sho·meir Yis·ra·eil,	שׁוֹמֵר יִשְׂרָאֵל,
She·mor she·ei·rit Yis·ra·eil,	שְׁמוֹר שְׁאֵרִית יִשְׂרָאֵל,
Ve·al yo·vad Yis·ra·eil,	וְאַל יֹאבַד יִשְׂרָאֵל,
Ha·o·me·rim, "She·ma Yis·ra·eil."	הָאוֹמְרִים "שְׁמַע יִשְׂרָאֵל."

Sho·meir goi e·chad,	שׁוֹמֵר גּוֹי אֶחָד,
She·mor she·ei·rit am e·chad.	שְׁמוֹר שְׁאֵרִית עַם אֶחָד,
Ve·al yo·vad goi e·chad,	וְאַל יֹאבַד גּוֹי אֶחָד,
Ha·me·ya·cha·dim shi·me·cha,	הַמְיַחֲדִים שִׁמְךָ,
"A·do·nai E·lo·hei·nu, A·do·nai e·chad."	"יְיָ אֱלֹהֵינוּ, יְיָ אֶחָד."

26

Guardian of Israel,
Guard the remnant of Israel.
May none perish in Israel,
The people that proclaims: Hear, O Israel.

Guardian of a unique people,
Guard the remnant of that people.
May none perish of the people
That proclaims: The Lord is our God, the Lord is One.

◇◇

WHO TURNS? THE HOUSE OF ISRAEL

To be a Jew in the twentieth century
Is to be offered a gift. If you refuse,
Wishing to be invisible, you choose
Death of the spirit, the stone insanity.
Accepting, take full life. Full agonies:
Your evening deep in labyrinthine blood
Of those who resist, fall, and resist; and God
Reduced to a hostage among hostages.

The gift is torment. Not alone the still
Torture, isolation; or torture of the flesh.
That may come also. But the accepting wish,
The whole and fertile spirit as guarantee
For every human freedom, suffering to be free,
Daring to live for the impossible.

◇◇

we Jews are as the dew,
on every blade of grass,
trodden under foot today
and here tomorrow morning.

◇◇

אִם־שָׁמוֹעַ תִּשְׁמְעוּ בְּקֹלִי וּשְׁמַרְתֶּם אֶת־בְּרִיתִי,
וִהְיִיתֶם לִי סְגֻלָּה מִכָּל־הָעַמִּים.
וְאַתֶּם תִּהְיוּ־לִי מַמְלֶכֶת כֹּהֲנִים, וְגוֹי קָדוֹשׁ.

If you truly listen to Me and keep My covenant, you shall
be My treasured possession among the peoples.

You shall be to Me a kingdom of priests, a holy people.

הֵן עַבְדִּי, אֶתְמָךְ־בּוֹ; בְּחִירִי, רָצְתָה נַפְשִׁי.
אַתֶּם עֵדַי, נְאֻם־יְיָ, וְעַבְדִּי אֲשֶׁר בָּחָרְתִּי.

Behold My servant, whom I uphold; My chosen, in whom
My soul delights.

You are My witnesses, says the Lord, and My chosen ser-
vant.

לִפְקֹחַ עֵינַיִם עִוְרוֹת, לְהוֹצִיא מִמַּסְגֵּר אַסִּיר, מִבֵּית
כֶּלֶא יֹשְׁבֵי חֹשֶׁךְ.
נָקֵל מִהְיוֹתְךָ לִי עֶבֶד לְהָקִים אֶת־שִׁבְטֵי יַעֲקֹב, וּנְצוּרֵי
יִשְׂרָאֵל לְהָשִׁיב:

To open blind eyes, to bring the captive out of the dun-
geon, those who sit in darkness out of their prison.

It is not enough that you should be My servant only to
re-establish the tribes of Jacob and to restore the survivors
of Israel:

28

וּנְתַתִּיךָ לְאוֹר גּוֹיִם, לִהְיוֹת יְשׁוּעָתִי עַד־קְצֵה הָאָרֶץ.
וְנִבְרְכוּ בְךָ כָּל־מִשְׁפְּחֹת הָאֲדָמָה, וּבְזַרְעֶךָ.

I will make you a light to the nations, that My deliverance
may reach to the ends of the earth.

*Through you and through your descendants shall all the
families of the earth be blessed.*

◇◇

MEDITATION

Being a Jew means running forever to God
Even if you are His betrayer,
Means expecting to hear any day,
Even if you are a nay sayer,
The blare of Messiah's horn;

Means, even if you wish to,
You cannot escape His snares,
You cannot cease to pray—
Even after all the prayers,
Even after all the "evens."

◇◇

29

THE GOD WE TURN TO

O incognito god, anonymous lord,
with what name shall I call you? Where shall I
discover the syllable, the mystic word
that shall invoke you from eternity?
is that sweet sound the heart makes, clocking life,
Your appellation? is the noise of thunder, it?
Is it the hush of peace, the sound of strife?

I have no title for your glorious throne,
and for your presence not a golden word,—
only that wanting you, by that alone,
I do invoke you, knowing I am heard.

◇◇

God, You taunt me: 'Flee if you can!'
But I can't flee,
For when I turn away from You, angry and heartsick,
With a vow on my lips like a burning coal:
'I will not see You again'—

I can't do it.
And I turn back
And knock on Your door,
Tortured with longing

As though You had sent me a love-letter.

◇◇

(Note: In our tradition, the Divine Presence [Shechinah] is feminine. And letters/numbers often point to hidden and ultimate truths.)

Mothering Presence
enfold me
unfold me
& walk with me.
& walk with me.

> I need to turn to You
> I need to walk with You
> I need to rest in You

Beloved come to me
but not to win my wars.
Beloved come to me
but not to make my peace.
Come, O Loved One,
but not to build my house.

> If only You will walk with me
> if only You will be with me
> if only You will shelter me.

Maker of arithmetic
Weaver of number-worlds
Redeemer of equalities
Mother of odd/Sister of even
Creator of Aleph/Author of Bet:

> If only You will walk with me
> if only You will shelter me
> if only You will be with me.

Do not tell me no,
do not tell me,
no, do not tell me NO!
Do not say my life adds up to naught.

> If only You will shelter me
> if only You will be with me
> if only You will walk with me.

Nor say that two & two are always four
and must be so,

> nor say because our hearts shall stop
> that love must end.

Tell me YES!
that two and two need not make four,
for five & seven will often do,
for now and then again and now again
the sum I ask is life.

> If only You will walk with me
> if only You will be with me
> if only You will be . . .

I swear that one & one are three:
I see it always so
when lovers kiss
& friends embrace.

> If only You will walk with me
> if only You will be . . .

YES!
Although my heart is stone.
YES!
Because my heart is stone.
I need to turn to You.

I need to hope in You
I need to turn to You
I need to rest in You.

Mother present in all
Mother present in all presence
in all whom I am present to:
move me, move all of us;
move head, move hand
with the promise of Your word
with the Presence of Your life.
Move the heart in us,
that stranger in our midst,
and let it turn to flesh from stone.

We need to turn to You
we need to walk with You
we need to rest in You.

So the garden planted,
garden planted in our wilderness
be safe from harm.
So the planted flowers bloom
while empires wither.
So You be our dwelling place
and we are free.

If only You will be with us
if only You will be . . .

◇◇

MEDITATIONS

Our God was to be a breath, and not a postcard
Of the sun setting over Niagara Falls:
"Wish you were here." Our God was first the breath
That raised a whirlwind in the desert dust,

The Wilderness of Sin. And then a word
Unspeakable, a stillness, and a standing stone
Set in the road; you would not raise a chisel
Upon that stone. Nothing but sky and sand
To purify a forbidden generation
Of Egypt's kitchens. In that wilderness
I've wandered for my forty years also,
Lifting mirages to break horizons, dreaming
Idolatries to alphabet the void,
Sending these postcards to the self at home:
Sunlight on pouring water; wish I were here.

◇

Something is very gently,
invisibly, silently,
pulling at me—a thread
or net of threads
finer than cobweb and as
elastic. I haven't tried
the strength of it. No barbed hook
pierced and tore me. Was it
not long ago this thread
began to draw me? Or
way back? Was I
born with its knot about my
neck, a bridle? Not fear
but a stirring
of wonder makes me
catch my breath when I feel
the tug of it when I thought
it had loosened itself and gone.

◇

The leaves fall, fall as from afar . . .
They fall with slow and lingering descent.
And in the nights the heavy earth, too, falls,
From out the stars into the Solitude.
Thus all must fall. This hand of mine must fall,
And lo! the other one:—it is the law.
But there is One who holds this falling
infinitely softly in His hands.

◇◇

THE HOUSE OF ISRAEL AND THE GOD OF ISRAEL

Who has plumbed the mind of the Lord,
who can instruct the Ancient of Days?
What likeness can you find for God,
what form resembles Me?
Why declare, O Israel,
'My way is hid from the Lord,
my cause is ignored by my God?'
Do you not know?
Have you not heard?
I, the Lord, am God from of old,
Creator of the earth from end to end;
I never grow faint or weary,
My wisdom cannot be fathomed.
I give strength to the faint,
fresh vigor to the spent.
Turn to Me and be saved,
all the ends of the earth!

The Lord is our chosen portion,
our cup of salvation;
our lines have fallen for us in pleasant places,
and our heritage is truly good.

◇

As clay takes form
in a potter's hand,
so do we in Yours.

Mold us into human form.
You are the potter;
we are but clay.

As words are shaped
by a poet's hand,
so are we by Yours.

Make us Your song.
You are the singer,
we are Your work.

As a ship takes its course
from a sailor's hand,
so do we from Yours.

Set us on Your chosen course.
You are the sailor;
we are Your ship.

As threads are patterned
by a weaver's hand,
so are we by Yours.

Weave us into Your plan, O God.
We are Your people;
You are our King!

◇◇

We are Your people,	כִּי אָנוּ עַמֶּךְ
You are our King.	וְאַתָּה מַלְכֵּנוּ.
We are Your children,	אָנוּ בָנֶיךָ
You are our Father.	וְאַתָּה אָבִינוּ.
We are Your possession,	אָנוּ נַחֲלָתֶךְ
You are our Portion.	וְאַתָּה גוֹרָלֵנוּ.
We are Your flock,	אָנוּ צֹאנֶךְ
You are our Shepherd.	וְאַתָּה רוֹעֵנוּ.
We are Your vineyard,	אָנוּ כַרְמֶךְ
You are our Keeper.	וְאַתָּה נוֹטְרֵנוּ.
We are Your beloved,	אָנוּ רַעְיָתֶךְ
You are our Friend.	וְאַתָּה דוֹדֵנוּ.

◇◇

THE DIVINE COMPASSION

אֵל מֶלֶךְ, יוֹשֵׁב עַל כִּסֵּא רַחֲמִים, מִתְנַהֵג בַּחֲסִידוּת,
מוֹחֵל עֲוֹנוֹת עַמּוֹ, מַעֲבִיר רִאשׁוֹן רִאשׁוֹן, מַרְבֶּה
מְחִילָה לַחַטָּאִים, וּסְלִיחָה לַפּוֹשְׁעִים. עוֹשֶׂה צְדָקוֹת
עִם כָּל בָּשָׂר וָרוּחַ, לֹא כְּרָעָתָם תִּגְמֹל.

Sovereign God, whose throne is mercy, You guide the
world with steadfast love, forgiving the transgressions of
Your people; You pardon all who sin, are generous with
all who live, treating them with compassion.

אֵל, הוֹרֵיתָ לָנוּ לוֹמַר שְׁלֹשׁ עֶשְׂרֵה. זְכֹר לָנוּ הַיּוֹם
בְּרִית שְׁלֹשׁ עֶשְׂרֵה, כְּמוֹ שֶׁהוֹדַעְתָּ לֶעָנָו מִקֶּדֶם, כְּמוֹ
שֶׁכָּתוּב: "וַיֵּרֶד יְיָ בֶּעָנָן, וַיִּתְיַצֵּב עִמּוֹ שָׁם, וַיִּקְרָא בְשֵׁם
יְיָ. וַיַּעֲבֹר יְיָ עַל פָּנָיו וַיִּקְרָא:

37

You have taught us, O God, Your covenant with life. This day remember Your covenant, revealed from of old to Moses, the humble one. As it is written: The Lord descended in a cloud and stood with him there and revealed the divine nature. The Lord passed before Moses and said:

יְיָ, יְיָ אֵל רַחוּם וְחַנּוּן, אֶרֶךְ אַפַּיִם וְרַב־חֶסֶד וֶאֱמֶת, נֹצֵר חֶסֶד לָאֲלָפִים, נֹשֵׂא עָוֹן וָפֶשַׁע וְחַטָּאָה וְנַקֵּה.

The Lord, the Lord God is merciful and gracious,

endlessly patient,

loving and true,

showing mercy to thousands,

forgiving our sin,

and granting pardon.

We pray with Moses:

Pardon our sin;	וְסָלַחְתָּ לַעֲוֹנֵנוּ
call us Your own,	וּלְחַטָּאתֵנוּ
call us Your own.	וּנְחַלְתָּנוּ.

◇◇

וִיהִי רָצוֹן מִלְּפָנֶיךָ, יְיָ אֱלֹהֵינוּ וֵאלֹהֵי אֲבוֹתֵינוּ, שֶׁתִּשְׁבֹּר וְתַשְׁבִּית עֻלּוֹ שֶׁל־יֵצֶר הָרַע מִלִּבֵּנוּ, שֶׁכָּךְ בְּרָאתָנוּ לַעֲשׂוֹת רְצוֹנֶךָ, וְאָנוּ חַיָּבִים לַעֲשׂוֹת רְצוֹנֶךָ. אַתְּ חָפֵץ וְאָנוּ חֲפֵצִים, וּמִי מְעַכֵּב? שְׂאוֹר שֶׁבָּעִסָּה.

38

גָּלוּי וְיָדוּעַ לְפָנֶיךָ שֶׁאֵין בָּנוּ כְּחַ לַעֲמוֹד בּוֹ, אֶלָּא יְהִי
רָצוֹן מִלְּפָנֶיךָ, יְיָ אֱלֹהֵינוּ וֵאלֹהֵי אֲבוֹתֵינוּ,
שֶׁתַּשְׁבִּיתֵהוּ מֵעָלֵינוּ וְתַכְנִיעֵהוּ, וְנַעֲשֶׂה רְצוֹנְךָ
כִּרְצוֹנֵנוּ בְּלֵבָב שָׁלֵם.

*Lord our God and God of all generations, help us to over-
come the impulse to do evil. You have created us able to do
Your will, but in our nature there is a wayward spirit that
hinders us and keeps us from doing what we should. O
Lord our God, help us to subdue it, so that we may, with a
whole heart, make Your will our own.*

◇◇

Ha·shi·vei·nu A·do·nai ei·le·cha,

ve·na·shu·vah.

cha·deish ya·mei·nu ke·ke·dem.

הֲשִׁיבֵנוּ יְיָ אֵלֶיךָ,

וְנָשׁוּבָה.

חַדֵּשׁ יָמֵינוּ כְּקֶדֶם.

Help us to return to You, O Lord: then truly shall we return.
Renew our days as in the past.

◇◇

Your mercy, O God of all life, extends to all who live. You
turn from our transgressions, that we may turn to You.
For You love all beings, despising nothing that You have
made. For how could You hate what You have established,
and what would endure without Your love? All things are
touched by Your grace, for they are Yours. Lord, You take
delight in life, for Your eternal spirit dwells in all that
breathes.

◇◇

שְׁמַע קוֹלֵנוּ, יְיָ אֱלֹהֵינוּ, חוּס וְרַחֵם עָלֵינוּ,
וְקַבֵּל בְּרַחֲמִים וּבְרָצוֹן אֶת־תְּפִלָּתֵנוּ.
הֲשִׁיבֵנוּ יְיָ אֵלֶיךָ, וְנָשׁוּבָה. חַדֵּשׁ יָמֵינוּ כְּקֶדֶם.
אֲמָרֵינוּ הַאֲזִינָה, יְיָ, בִּינָה הֲגִיגֵנוּ.
אַל תַּשְׁלִיכֵנוּ מִלְּפָנֶיךָ, וְרוּחַ קָדְשְׁךָ אַל תִּקַּח מִמֶּנּוּ.
אַל תַּשְׁלִיכֵנוּ לְעֵת זִקְנָה, כִּכְלוֹת כֹּחֵנוּ אַל תַּעַזְבֵנוּ.
אַל תַּעַזְבֵנוּ, יְיָ אֱלֹהֵינוּ, אַל תִּרְחַק מִמֶּנּוּ.
כִּי לְךָ, יְיָ, הוֹחָלְנוּ, אַתָּה תַעֲנֶה, אֲדֹנָי אֱלֹהֵינוּ.

Hear our voice, Lord our God; have compassion upon us,
and with that compassion accept our prayer.

*Help us to return to You, O Lord; then truly shall we
return. Renew our days as of old.*

Consider our words, Lord: look into our inmost thoughts.

*Do not cast us away from Your presence, do not remove
Your holy spirit.*

Do not dismiss us when we are old; as our strength dimin-
ishes, do not abandon us.

Do not abandon us, Lord our God; do not be far from us.

For You, Lord, do we wait; and You, our God, will answer.

◇◇

WE ACKNOWLEDGE OUR SINS

אֱלֹהֵינוּ וֵאלֹהֵי אֲבוֹתֵינוּ, תָּבֹא לְפָנֶיךָ תְּפִלָּתֵנוּ. וְאַל
תִּתְעַלַּם מִתְּחִנָּתֵנוּ, שֶׁאֵין אֲנַחְנוּ עַזֵּי פָנִים וּקְשֵׁי עֹרֶף,
לוֹמַר לְפָנֶיךָ, יְיָ אֱלֹהֵינוּ וֵאלֹהֵי אֲבוֹתֵינוּ, צַדִּיקִים

אֲנַחְנוּ וְלֹא חָטָאנוּ; אֲבָל אֲנַחְנוּ חָטָאנוּ; חָטָאנוּ,
עָוִינוּ, פָּשָׁעְנוּ.

Our God, God of our mothers and fathers, grant that our
prayers may reach You. Do not be deaf to our pleas, for
we are not so arrogant and stiff-necked as to say before
You, Lord our God and God of all ages, we are perfect and
have not sinned; rather do we confess: we have gone
astray, we have sinned, we have transgressed.

SHORT CONFESSION   וידוי זוטא

אָשַׁמְנוּ, בָּגַדְנוּ, גָזַלְנוּ, דִּבַּרְנוּ דֹפִי.
הֶעֱוִינוּ, וְהִרְשַׁעְנוּ, זַדְנוּ, חָמַסְנוּ,
טָפַלְנוּ שֶׁקֶר. יָעַצְנוּ רָע, כִּזַּבְנוּ, לַצְנוּ,
מָרַדְנוּ, נִאַצְנוּ, סָרַרְנוּ, עָוִינוּ,
פָּשַׁעְנוּ, צָרַרְנוּ, קִשִּׁינוּ עֹרֶף. רָשַׁעְנוּ,
שִׁחַתְנוּ, תִּעַבְנוּ, תָּעִינוּ, תִּעְתָּעְנוּ.

We all have committed offenses; together we confess these
human sins:

*The sins of arrogance, bigotry, and cynicism; of deceit and
egotism, flattery and greed, injustice and jealousy.*

Some of us kept grudges, were lustful, malicious, or
narrow-minded.

*Others were obstinate or possessive, quarrelsome, rancor-
ous, or selfish.*

There was violence, weakness of will, xenophobia:

We yielded to temptation, and showed zeal for bad causes.

41

וּבְכֵן יְהִי רָצוֹן מִלְפָנֶיךָ, יְיָ אֱלֹהֵינוּ וֵאלֹהֵי אֲבוֹתֵינוּ, שֶׁתִּסְלַח לָנוּ עַל כָּל־חַטֹּאתֵינוּ וְתִמְחַל לָנוּ עַל כָּל־עֲוֹנוֹתֵינוּ וּתְכַפֶּר־לָנוּ עַל כָּל־פְּשָׁעֵינוּ.

Now may it be Your will, O Lord God of all the generations, to pardon all our sins, to forgive all our wrongdoings, and to blot out all our transgressions:

LONG CONFESSION   וידוי רבה

עַל חֵטְא

עַל חֵטְא שֶׁחָטָאנוּ לְפָנֶיךָ בְּאֹנֶס וּבְרָצוֹן.

The sin we have committed against You under duress or by choice.

עַל חֵטְא שֶׁחָטָאנוּ לְפָנֶיךָ בְּזָדוֹן וּבִשְׁגָגָה.

The sin we have committed against You consciously or unconsciously.

וְעַל חֵטְא שֶׁחָטָאנוּ לְפָנֶיךָ בַּגָּלוּי וּבַסָּתֶר.

And the sin we have committed against You openly or secretly.

עַל חֵטְא שֶׁחָטָאנוּ לְפָנֶיךָ בְּשִׂנְאַת חִנָּם.

The sin we have committed against You by hating without cause.

עַל חֵטְא שֶׁחָטָאנוּ לְפָנֶיךָ בְּמַשָּׂא וּבְמַתָּן.

The sin we have committed against You by dishonesty in business.

42

וְעַל חֵטְא שֶׁחָטָאנוּ לְפָנֶיךָ בְּהוֹנָאַת רֵעַ.

And the sin we have committed against You by hurting others in any way.

Ve·al ku·lam, E·lo·ah
se·li·chot, se·lach la·nu,
me·chal la·nu, ka·per la·nu!

וְעַל כֻּלָּם, אֱלְוֹהַּ
סְלִיחוֹת, סְלַח לָנוּ,
מְחַל לָנוּ, כַּפֶּר־לָנוּ!

For all these, O God of mercy, forgive us, pardon us, grant us atonement!

◇◇

עַל חֵטְא שֶׁחָטָאנוּ לְפָנֶיךָ . . .

We have sinned against life by failing to work for peace.

We have sinned against life by keeping silent in the face of injustice.

עַל חֵטְא שֶׁחָטָאנוּ לְפָנֶיךָ . . .

We have sinned against life by ignoring those who suffer in distant lands.

We have sinned against life by forgetting the poor in our own midst.

עַל חֵטְא שֶׁחָטָאנוּ לְפָנֶיךָ . . .

We have failed to respect those made in the image of God.

We have withheld our love from those who depend on us.

43

עַל חֵטְא שֶׁחָטָאנוּ לְפָנֶיךָ . . .

We have engaged in gossip and in repeated slander.

We have distorted the truth for our own advantage.

עַל חֵטְא שֶׁחָטָאנוּ לְפָנֶיךָ . . .

We have conformed to fashion and not to conscience.

We have indulged in despair and trafficked with cynics.

עַל חֵטְא שֶׁחָטָאנוּ לְפָנֶיךָ . . .

We have given meager support to our Houses of Study.

We have neglected our heritage of learning.

עַל חֵטְא שֶׁחָטָאנוּ לְפָנֶיךָ . . .

We have sinned against ourselves and paid scant heed to the life of the spirit.

We have sinned against ourselves and have not risen to fulfill the best that is in us.

Ve·al ku·lam, E·lo·ah
se·li·chot, se·lach la·nu,
me·chal la·nu, ka·per la·nu!

וְעַל כֻּלָּם, אֱלוֹהַּ
סְלִיחוֹת, סְלַח לָנוּ,
מְחַל לָנוּ, כַּפֶּר-לָנוּ!

For all these, O God of mercy, forgive us, pardon us, grant us atonement!

◇◇

44

God before whom words must be true, we acknowledge our faults and our failings. Help us now to strengthen the good impulse within us.

Help us to care about wrongs from which we have been spared; to seek forgiveness for the wrongs we shall do; to forgive the wrongs that are done to us.

Create in us a clean heart, and place a willing spirit within us.

Shed Your light upon us, O God, that we may see the goodness in each of Your children.

◇◇

MEDITATION

Keep me, O God, from bad intentions and from excessive pride; help me at all times to govern my passions and master my inclinations. Against melancholy and bitterness defend my soul; guard my tongue against slander and deceit, and open my eyes to the virtues of others.

◇◇

A·vi·nu· mal·kei·nu, cho·nei·nu	אָבִינוּ מַלְכֵּינוּ, חָנֵּנוּ
va·a·nei·nu, ki ein ba·nu	וַעֲנֵנוּ, כִּי אֵין בָּנוּ
ma·a·sim, a sei i·ma·nu	מַעֲשִׂים, עֲשֵׂה עִמָּנוּ
tse·da·kah va·che·sed, ve·ho·shi·ei·nu.	צְדָקָה וָחֶסֶד, וְהוֹשִׁיעֵנוּ.

Our Father, our King, be gracious and answer us, even when we have little merit; treat us generously and with kindness, and be our help.

◇◇

45

IN GOD'S PRESENCE

Before the open Ark

אֱלֹהֵינוּ שֶׁבַּשָּׁמַיִם, דְּרַשְׁנוּךָ: הִמָּצֵא־לָנוּ.

Our God above, we seek You; grant that we may find You.

אֱלֹהֵינוּ שֶׁבַּשָּׁמַיִם, גַּלֵּה כְּבוֹד מַלְכוּתְךָ עָלֵינוּ.

Our God above, reveal to us the glory of Your kingdom.

אֱלֹהֵינוּ שֶׁבַּשָּׁמַיִם, קָרְבֵנוּ לַעֲבֹדָתֶךָ.

Our God above, draw us near to Your service.

אֱלֹהֵינוּ שֶׁבַּשָּׁמַיִם, צַוֵּה אִתָּנוּ בִרְכוֹתֶיךָ.

Our God above, grant us Your blessings.

אֱלֹהֵינוּ שֶׁבַּשָּׁמַיִם, צַוֵּה אִתָּנוּ יְשׁוּעוֹתֶיךָ.

Our God above, help us with Your saving acts.

אֱלֹהֵינוּ שֶׁבַּשָּׁמַיִם, שִׁית שָׁלוֹם בֵּינֵינוּ.

Our God above, let peace reign among us.

אֱלֹהֵינוּ שֶׁבַּשָּׁמַיִם, תֵּן שָׁלוֹם בָּאָרֶץ.

Our God above, grant peace to the earth.

אֱלֹהֵינוּ שֶׁבַּשָּׁמַיִם, תֵּן שֹׂבָע בְּעוֹלָמָךְ.

Our God above, grant abundance to Your world.

אֱלֹהֵינוּ שֶׁבַּשָּׁמַיִם, קָרֵב לָנוּ קֵץ הַגְּאֻלָּה.

Our God above, hasten for us the day of redemption.

◇◇

מִתְרַצֶּה בְּרַחֲמִים וּמִתְפַּיֵּס בְּתַחֲנוּנִים,
הִתְרַצֵּה וְהִתְפַּיֵּס לְדוֹר עָנִי, כִּי אֵין עוֹזֵר.

We pray for compassion and plead for grace. O God our Help, favor us and grant us peace.

אָבִינוּ מַלְכֵּנוּ, חָנֵּנוּ וַעֲנֵנוּ, כִּי אֵין בָּנוּ מַעֲשִׂים, עֲשֵׂה עִמָּנוּ צְדָקָה וָחֶסֶד וְהוֹשִׁיעֵנוּ.

Our Father, our King, be gracious and answer us, even when we have little merit; treat us generously and with kindness, and be our help.

וַאֲנַחְנוּ לֹא נֵדַע מַה נַּעֲשֶׂה, כִּי עָלֶיךָ עֵינֵינוּ.
זְכֹר רַחֲמֶיךָ, יְיָ, וַחֲסָדֶיךָ, כִּי מֵעוֹלָם הֵמָּה.

Uncertain of our ways, we look to You. Remember Your compassion and Your steadfast love, O Lord, for they are eternal.

יְהִי חַסְדְּךָ, יְיָ, עָלֵינוּ, כַּאֲשֶׁר יִחַלְנוּ לָךְ.
אַל תִּזְכָּר לָנוּ עֲוֹנוֹת רִאשֹׁנִים.
מַהֵר יְקַדְּמוּנוּ רַחֲמֶיךָ, כִּי דַלּוֹנוּ מְאֹד.

Lord, for You alone we wait in hope; extend to us Your grace. Let not past errors be held against us; when our own merits are few, let Your compassion be quick to meet us.

47

חָנֵּנוּ, יְיָ, חָנֵּנוּ, כִּי רַב שָׂבַעְנוּ בוּז. בְּרֹגֶז רַחֵם תִּזְכּוֹר.
כִּי הוּא יָדַע יִצְרֵנוּ, זָכוּר כִּי עָפָר אֲנָחְנוּ.

Be gracious, Lord, be gracious to us; our cup of sorrows is
full: behold us with compassion. Remember how we are
made; remember that we are dust.

עָזְרֵנוּ, אֱלֹהֵי יִשְׁעֵנוּ, עַל דְּבַר כְּבוֹד שְׁמֶךָ,
וְהַצִּילֵנוּ וְכַפֵּר עַל חַטֹּאתֵינוּ לְמַעַן שְׁמֶךָ.

*O God our Help, as Your nature is Your glory, save us;
help us atone for our sins, that Your will may prevail.*

◇◇

Ha·shi·vei·nu A·do·nai ei·le·cha,

ve·na·shu·vah.

cha·deish ya·mei·nu ke·ke·dem.

הֲשִׁיבֵנוּ יְיָ אֵלֶיךָ,
וְנָשׁוּבָה.
חַדֵּשׁ יָמֵינוּ כְּקֶדֶם.

Help us to return to You, O Lord; then truly shall we return.
Renew our days as in the past.

◇◇

תקיעה גדולה

TEKIAH GEDOLAH

NOTES AND ACKNOWLEDGMENTS

Introduction

The purpose of these notes is to identify the sources of the prayers and meditations contained in *Shaarei Selichah, Gates of Forgiveness;* to draw attention to, and explain, any textual changes that have been made, as well as features of the translation that require special comment; and to acknowledge the sources of copyrighted passages.

The liturgy of the Synagogue, and especially of the Reform movement in Judaism, is characterized by an extraordinary stylistic diversity, deriving from the vast span of time during which it was composed. This volume is no exception. It contains passages from the Bible, and thus from the earliest period of Jewish creativity, and alongside them is poetry and prose written as recently as 1978. In spite of this diversity, there is a pervading unity, partly because of the abundant use that has been made in every period of the Bible and its language, and even more because of the *basically* unchanged and unchanging universe of ideas and aspirations expressed in the liturgy.

As indicated in the Introduction, there has not been an 'official' Selichot Service in the Reform movement. This volume, therefore, breaks new ground in the development of the liturgy. The Editor has drawn upon the traditional prayers of Selichot, but has taken the opportunity to offer an innovative service, both in form and content.

The Editor wishes to thank all who contributed suggestions and criticism. They include the following members of the Liturgy Committee of the Central Conference of American Rabbis who served through June, 1979: A. Stanley Dreyfus (Chairman until June, 1979), Lawrence A. Hoffman (Chairman

49

since June, 1979), Jay R. Brickman, Herbert Bronstein, Harvey J. Fields, Norman D. Hirsh, Gunter Hirschberg, and Frederic S. Pomerantz. In addition to the above named, the following served as *ex-officio* members of the Liturgy Committee and participated in its deliberations: Joseph B. Glaser, W. Gunther Plaut, Malcolm H. Stern, and Elliot L. Stevens. George Weinflash served as delegate for the American Conference of Cantors. Edward Graham made a number of helpful suggestions.

Chaim Stern

Abbreviations

BOOKS OF THE BIBLE

N.B. The references are to the Hebrew (Masoretic) division into chapters and verses, as maintained in Jewish translations of the Bible; Christian translations may differ slightly in this respect.

CHRON.	Chronicles
DEUT.	Deuteronomy
DAN.	Daniel
EXOD.	Exodus
EZEK.	Ezekiel
GEN.	Genesis
HOS.	Hosea
ISA.	Isaiah
LAM.	Lamentations
LEV.	Leviticus
NEH.	Nehemiah
NUM.	Numbers
PS., PSS.	Psalm, Psalms
ZECH.	Zechariah

OTHER ABBREVIATIONS

Abrahams	Dr. Israel Abrahams (1858-1925), *A Companion to the Authorised Daily Prayer Book*, Hermon Press, N.Y., 1966 (first published 1922).
B.	Babylonian Talmud
b.	ben (son of)
B.C.E.	Before the Common Era
Ber.	Berachot (tractate of Mishnah, Tosefta, or Talmud)
C.	Century (Common Era, unless otherwise stated)
c.	*circa*
CCAR	Central Conference of American Rabbis
C.E.	Common Era

cf.	Compare
CS	Rabbi Chaim Stern
ed.	edited, edition, editor
e.g.	for example
f., ff.	following (one or two pages)
GOR	*Gate of Repentance* (ULPS, London, 1973)
Ibid.	In the same place
Idelsohn	Dr. Abraham Z. Idelsohn (1882-1938), *Jewish Liturgy and its Development*, Schocken Books, N.Y., 1967 (first published 1932).
J.	'Jerusalem' Talmud
JE	*The Jewish Encyclopedia*, Funk and Wagnalls Company, N.Y. and London, 1901
JR	Rabbi John D. Rayner
Levi	Eliezer Levi: *Yesodot Hatefillah* (1961 ed.)
lit.	literal, literally
LJPB	*Liberal Jewish Prayer Book* (vols. I and III, 1937 and 1926 eds.), ed. Israel I. Mattuck
M.	Mishnah
Meg.	Megillah (tractate of Mishnah, Tosefta, or Talmud)
MV	Machzor Vitry
No.	number
op. cit.	in the work cited
p., pp.	page, pages
Pal.	Palestinian
PB	prayerbook
R.	Rabbi, Rav
RH	Rosh Hashanah (tractate of Mishnah, Tosefta, or Talmud)
Rosenfeld	*The Authorised Selichot for the Whole Year*, trsl. and annotated by Rev. Abraham Rosenfeld, London, 1962
Soferim	'Minor Tractate' Soferim
SOH	*Service of the Heart* (1967), ed. CS and JR
SRA	*Seder Rav Amram Gaon*, ed. Daniel Goldschmidt, Hotza'at ha-Rav Kook, Jerusalem, 1971

ST	*Shaarei Tefillah (Gates of Prayer)*, CCAR, New York, 1975
trad.	tradition, traditional, traditionally
trsl.	translated by, translation, translator
ULPS	Union of Liberal and Progressive Synagogues (London)
UPB	*The Union Prayerbook for Jewish Worship*, Newly Revised, Part I, 1940; Part II, 1945. The latter is indicated as UPB II.
v.,vv.	verse, verses
vol.	volume

No. Page

HAVDALAH

1 3 *Behold, God is my Deliverer* . . . This is the opening of the Havdalah ritual, read at the conclusion of Shabbat, which we include because Selichot always begins on a Saturday evening. The word *Havdalah* means 'separation' or 'differentiation' and refers especially to the ritual of 'ushering out' the Sabbath or a Festival. This custom seems to be as ancient as the *Kiddush*, going back to Pharisaic times (Cf., e.g., M. Ber. 8.5 and Tosefta Ber. 6.7). There is some variation among the rituals as to the introductory Scriptural passages for the *Havdalah*. We offer the following: Isa. 12.2f. (we have assumed that the word זמרת trad. rendered 'song,' is to be understood in the light of a cognate Arabic word meaning 'to protect,' and we have therefore trsl. it 'shield.' See D. Winton Thomas in *Record and Revelation*, ed. by H. Wheeler Robinson, pp. 395ff.; we have also slightly adapted the trsl. of several vv., changing persons where it seemed necessary on grounds of English style); Pss. 3.9; 46.12; 84.13; 20.10; Esther 8.16; Ps. 116.13. The custom of prefacing the *Havdalah* ceremony with these Scriptural verses or a similar selection goes back to the 9th C. The accent is on *salvation* because the Messiah (or his forerunner, Elijah) was popularly expected to come following a Sabbath (on the Sabbath itself, which is a foretaste of the Messianic time, he would be redundant!), at the first opportunity, as the new week begins (Cf. Abrahams, p. 182).

2 4 *Blessed is the Lord . . . fruit of the vine.* M. Ber. 8.5-8 refers to this and the other *Havdalah* benedictions; Tosefta Ber. 6.7 (cited in B. Ber. 52a) mentions all three: wine, light, and spices. The benediction itself, recited before drinking wine, is mentioned in M. Ber. 6.1 as applying to all occasions.

3 4 *Blessed is the Lord . . . all the spices.* See preceding Note.

No. Page

The text of the benediction is cited in B. Ber. 43a. The use of spices in this context may go back to an ancient domestic custom, of bringing spices on burning coals into the room at the end of a meal (Cf. M. Ber. 6.6); this could, of course, only be done when the Sabbath was over (Cf. Levi, p. 204). Maimonides explains the custom as intended to 'cheer up' the 'additional soul' which, according to Rabbinic legend, dwells within the Jew during the Sabbath (B. Beitsah 16a; B. Ta-anit 27b); that 'over-soul' is saddened when the Sabbath departs, for it, in turn, must leave the Jew (*Mishneh Torah, Hilchot Shabbat* 29.29).

4   4   *Blessed is the Lord . . . the light of fire.* Lit., 'lights.' Because of the plural, it is customary to use a twisted candle, with two or more wicks (Cf. B. Pesachim 103b). The benediction is cited in M. Ber. 8.5 as that recommended by the school of Hillel. The custom of lighting a candle at the conclusion of the Sabbath is probably due to the desire to kindle light as soon as the Sabbath, during which the kindling of fire was prohibited, was over. It has also been connected with the story of creation; in this view, the blessing of light at the start of the first day commemorates the first day of creation, whose feature was the creation of light (Cf. Gen. Rabbah 12.5; B. Pesachim 53b). It may also be connected with the legend that Adam was frightened when it grew dark at the end of the Sabbath, whereupon God taught him how to kindle a fire (B. Pesachim 54a; cf. Levi, p. 204).

5   5   *Blessed is . . . who separates . . .* This is the principal benediction of the *Havdalah*, from which its name is derived. It is cited in B. Pesachim 103b. Scriptural allusions include Gen. 4.1 and 2.1-3.

6   5   *Elijah! Week after week . . .* New, by CS.

7   6   *Eiliyahu Hanavi . . .* A trad. folk song that has become asso-

No. Page

ciated with Pesach and with the *Havdalah*, on account of their connection with the figure of Elijah and the theme of redemption.

8   7   *You separate sacred from profane* . . . An abridged version of a poem with an acrostic indicating that it was written by 'Isaac the Little,' whom it is, however, not possible to identify with certainty. It may have been R. Isaac ibn Giyyat (11th C. Spain; cf. F. L. Cohen in JE, Vol. VI, p. 187). It was probably intended originally for the concluding service of Yom Kippur; hence its penitential tenor.

MEDITATIONS

9   11   *God does not want* . . . By Martin Buber (Austria/ Germany/Palestine/Israel, 1878-1965), one of the leading Jewish thinkers of the 20th C. From *Reden über das Judentum* ('Talks about Judaism'), Schocken Books, Berlin, 1932, p. 123.

10   11   *Religion is essentially* . . . From *Eclipse of God*, by Martin Buber (See No. 9). Harper & Brothers, Publishers, N.Y., 1952, p. 159. Trsl. by Maurice S. Friedman.

11   11   *It is not necessary* . . . *Ibid.*, p. 40. Slightly adapted by CS.

12   11   *We can speak* . . . From *The Essence of Judaism*, by Leo Baeck, (Germany/England, 1873-1956). Rabbi Baeck was the heroic leader of German Jewry throughout the Hitler period, a great teacher and expositor of Liberal Judaism. Schocken Books, Inc., N.Y., Revised Edition, 1948, p. 92. Slightly adapted by CS.

13   11   *The best worship* . . . Solomon ibn Gabirol (Spain, c. 1021-1058, poet and philosopher).

No. Page

14   11   *"I am prayer . . ." . . .* New, by CS.

15   12   *The Jews . . .* By Leo Baeck, *op. cit.*, p. 11.

16   12   *The Jew is . . . Ibid.*, p. 261. Slightly adapted by CS.

17   12   *It requires religious courage . . . Ibid.*, p. 274. Slightly adapted by CS.

18   12   *Jewish History . . . Ibid.*, pp. 139f. Slightly adapted by CS.

19   13   *The Torah . . .* B. Ber. 25b, 31a.

20   13   *Is there a truth . . .* A composite passage drawn from *Israel and the World* (Schocken Books, Inc., N.Y., 1948), p. 46, and from *The Origin and Meaning of Hasidism* (Horizon Press, N.Y., 1960), p. 229. Both are by Martin Buber (See No. 9). Slightly adapted by CS.

21   13   *Our life is fulfilled. . .* By Leo Baeck, *op. cit.*, p. 19.

22   13   *Whoever bears . . . Ibid.*, p. 152.

23   13   *If you wish . . .* Sifra on Lev. 19.15.

24   13   *The kingdom of God . . .* By Leo Baeck, *op. cit.*, p. 221.

25   13   *Every ethical deed . . . Ibid.*, p. 172.

26   14   *One does not . . .* From 'The Two Foci of the Jewish Soul,' in *Israel and the World* (See No. 9), by Martin Buber. Slightly adapted by CS.

27   14   *If you divide . . .* From *The Origin and Meaning of Hasidism*, p. 98, by Martin Buber (See No. 9). Slightly adapted by CS.

No. Page

28 14 *They are most* ... By Abraham ibn Ezra (Spain, 1092-1167). Quoted in *Forms of Prayer for Jewish Worship, I* (Reform Synagogues of Great Britain, London, 1977), p. 369, and here given in slightly different form.

29 14 *To love somebody* ... From *The Art of Loving*, by Erich Fromm. Harper & Row, Inc., 1974.

30 14 *Of all qualities* ... By the Chasidic master, Chenoch of Alexander (1798-1870).

31 15 *You may give* ... B. Bava Batra.

32 15 *The most beautiful* ... By Eleazar ben Judah of Worms (c. 1165-1238), from his ethical-mystical book, *Rokeach*.

33 15 *Days are scrolls* ... From *Chovot Halevavot* ('Duties of the Heart'), by Bachya ibn Pakuda (Spain c. 1050-1120). This volume is one of the most influential ethical works in Jewish literature.

34 15 *I am afraid* ... Kohelet Rabbah 8.

35 15 *I am afraid* ... Adapted by CS from *Forms of Prayer* ... (See No. 28), p. 373, where it is given as a Chasidic saying.

36 15 *Existence will remain* ... From *At the Turning*, by Martin Buber. Farrar, Straus & Young, N.Y., 1952, p. 44.

37 15 *Only an existence* ... By Leo Baeck, *op. cit.*, p. 83.

38 16 *Only when atonement* ... *Ibid.*, pp. 171f.

39 16 *The men and women in the Bible* ... From *Israel and the World* (See No. 20), p. 247, by Martin Buber. Slightly adapted by CS.

No. Page

40 16 *The older we get* . . . From *Nachlese* ('Afterwords') by Martin Buber. Verlag Lambert Schneider, Heidelberg, 1965, p. 254. Trsl. by Eva Jospe.

41 17 *We know nothing about death* . . . *Ibid.*, p. 127. Adapted slightly by CS.

SELICHOT

42 21 *Shabbat has ended* . . . From the trad. *Selichot.* Cf. Rosenfeld, p. 13. This is a medieval poem of uncertain authorship, attributed to an otherwise unidentified 'Samuel.' It is an alphabetical acrostic with the letter *Samech* missing. Freely trsl. by A. Stanley Dreyfus.

43 23 *Now is the time* . . . By Jack Riemer, in *New Prayers for the High Holy Days* (1970, 1971, Prayer Book Press of Media Judaica, Inc.). See *Gates of Repentance* (CCAR,1978), p. 372.

44 24 *Help us to return* . . . Lam. 5.21.

45 24 *Eternal God, what can we say* . . . From *Gates of Repentance*, p. 374, where it was new, by CS. Based on his prayer in GOR, p. 31.

46 25 *I have been one acquainted with the night* . . . A sonnet, 'Acquainted with the Night,' by Robert Frost. First used in our liturgy by CS in SOH, p. 234. See also ST, p. 670.

47 25 *Return, O Israel* . . . New, by CS. Incorporates the ff. Scriptural verses: Hos. 14.2 (adapted); Isa. 30.15; 25.4; 29.14a; 28.5a (adapted).

48 27 *Guardian of Israel* . . . A medieval poem of unknown authorship and uncertain date, possibly from the 13th C., first found in connection with Fast Days, and later

No. Page

added to the *Tachanun* (penitential prayers) for the weekday service. In the Sefardi Ritual, and in some others, this is found, with some variations, in the *Selichot* for the Ten Days of Repentance. See Idelsohn, p. 112. Nowadays, it is utilized as well in the Ashkenazi *Selichot*. See Rosenfeld, p. 22.

49 27 *To be a Jew in the twentieth century* . . . From Muriel Rukeyser, *Letter to the Front*. First used in our liturgy by CS in SOH, pp. 261f. See also ST, p. 706.

50 27 *We Jews* . . . From Charles Reznikoff, *In Memoriam: 1993*, The Objectivist Press, Copyright 1934 by publisher.

51 28 *If you truly listen to Me* . . . Exod. 19.5f; Isa. 42.1a; 43.10; 42.7; 49.6; Gen. 28.14b. First used in our liturgy by CS in SOH, pp. 259f. See also ST, pp. 703f. A not dissimilar reading appears in UPB I, p. 332.

52 29 *Being a Jew* . . . By Aaron Zeitlin, trsl. by Robert Friend. From *A Treasury of Yiddish Poetry*, ed. by Irving Howe and Eliezer Greenberg (Holt, Rinehart and Winston, N.Y., 1972). Copyright 1969 by the editors.

53 30 *O incognito god* . . . By A.M. Klein, 'Psalm XXIV,' in *Poems* (Jewish Publication Society of America, Philadelphia, 1944), p. 30. See also ST, p. 663.

54 30 *God, You taunt me* . . . Adapted by CS from a poem by Uri Zvi Greenberg trsl. by Robert Mezey and Ben Zion Gold, in *Poems from the Hebrew*, selected by Robert Mezey, (Thomas Y. Crowell Company, N.Y.) pp. 90f. Copyright 1973 by the editor. Hebrew copyright by ACUM, Ltd. of Tel-Aviv.

55 31 *Note: In our tradition* . . . New, by CS.

No. Page

56 31 *Mothering Presence* . . . New, by CS. Copyright 1979 by
CS.

57 33 *Our God* . . . A poem, 'The View from Pisgah,' by Howard
Nemerov, from *The Next Room of the Dream: Poems and
Two Plays* (Univ. of Chicago Press, 1962). Copyright 1962
by Howard Nemerov. For the *Wilderness of Sin,* see *Ency-
clopedia Judaica,* vol. 16, 512f.

58 34 *Something is very gently* . . . By Denise Levertov
(Goodman), 'The Thread' (New Directions, Publishers,
N.Y., 1958, 1961). Copyright 1958, 1961 by Denise Lever-
tov Goodman.

59 34 *The leaves fall* . . .By Rainer Maria Rilke, a poem,
'Autumn,' in *Sonnets from Orpheus* (1922), trsl. by Jesse
Lamont in *1001 Poems of Mankind,* ed. by H.W. Wells
(Tupper & Love, Atlanta), p. 211. First used in our liturgy
by CS in GOR, p. 390. See also *Gates of Repentance*
(CCAR, 1978), p. 489.

60 35 *Who has plumbed* . . . Freely adapted and trsl. by CS from
Isa. 40.13, 18, 27ff.; 45.22; Ps. 16.5f.

61 36 *As clay takes form* . . . A free variation by CS on the
anonymous *piyyut* (liturgical poem) *Ki Hinei Kachomer*
('As clay') for the Yom Kippur evening service and, more
generally, for the penitential season. It is thought to date
from 12th C.France, and is based, perhaps, on Jer. 18.6; Isa.
64.7. Cf. *Gates of Repentance,* pp. 381f. Michael Hecht has
written a not dissimilar variation on the theme of this poem.

62 37 *We are Your people* . . . A medieval poem, based on a passage in Song of Songs Rabbah 2.16, which cites a Scriptural
proof-text for each clause. Our version is abridged; the
trad. one has twelve units.

No. Page

63 37 *Sovereign God . . .* Included in some ms.of R. Amram Gaon (9th C. head of the Babylonian academy at Sura). Cf. Rosenfeld, p. 9, and SRA, p. 147.

64 38 *You have taught us . . .* This is a continuation of the preceding passage. It concludes by quoting Exod. 34.5.

65 38 *The Lord, the Lord God . . .* Exodus 34.6f. This passage is known as the 'Thirteen Attributes (of God).' This designation, as well as the liturgical use of this passage, is attested in B. RH 17b in the name of the 3rd C. Pal. Amora, R. Yochanan of Nappacha. See SRA, p. 147. Trad., it is here recited three times. Our text is trad., following ST, p. 392 and *Gates of Repentance*, p. 338. UPB II (p. 65) and GOR (p. 76) cut the text short by one word. The Biblical text, from which this passage is extracted, concludes with the words *Venakei lo yenakeh*, 'Yet (God) will not fully pardon (the guilty).' The Rabbis reversed the meaning of this Scriptural passage by omitting the last two words, thus yielding, as in our text, 'and granting pardon.' This, in our view, is a salutary instance of the compassionate independence of thought manifested by the Rabbis, and we therefore retain the word omitted by the other Reform liturgies mentioned above.

66 38 *We pray with Moses . . .* Exod. 34.9b. The first four English words are added by us for the sake of continuity.

67 39 *Lord our God . . . our own.* From ST, p. 391. This is a prayer by R. Tanchuma b. Skolastikai, cited in J. Ber. 4.2. Our trsl. is slightly abridged.

68 39 *Help us to return . . .* Lam. 5.21.

69 39 *Your mercy, O God . . .* Adapted by CS from a Hebrew trsl. of The Wisdom of Solomon 11.23-12.1, by A. Kahana, in *Ha-Sefarim ha-Hitsonim* ('The Apocrypha').

No. Page

70 40 *Hear our voice* . . . From the trad. *Selichot*. Cf. Rosenfeld, p. 16, where it is dated as coming from the 16th C. The first verse, however, is (in slightly abridged form) in SRA, p. 153. This verse also begins the last of the intermediate benedictions of the weekday *Tefillah*, and it is mentioned in the Talmud, B. Meg. 18a. The remaining verses are Biblical: Lam. 5.21; Pss. 5.2; 51.13; 71.9; 38.22, 17. A number of the verses are changed to the plural already by trad. Our version is somewhat abridged and rearranged. See *Gates of Repentance*, pp. 278f.

71 41 *Our God* . . . *all our transgressions.* These are the opening paragraphs of the *Viddui*, 'Confession of Sin.' As an established feature of the Yom Kippur liturgy, the Confession is first alluded to in the Tosefta, *Yom Hakippurim* 5.14, where it is prescribed throughout the day. The Talmud (Yoma 87b) mentions several versions, including a phrase from the present one. The full text is in SRA, p. 160. As regards its use for *Selichot*, SRA, p. 153, has the one phrase from the Talmud. We trsl. אלהינו ואלהי אבותינו (lit., 'Our God and God of our fathers') somewhat freely, to avoid exclusive use of the masculine. The second English passage, beginning 'We all have committed,' is a new version by CS of the catalogue of sins which in the Hebrew takes the form of an alphabetical acrostic. It (the English) omits several letters of the alphabet. Cf. GOR, p. 215, which has an alphabetical acrostic by JR that influenced the present version. And see *Gates of Repentance*, pp. 269f., 270.

72 42 *The sin we have committed* . . . This is a sharply abridged version of *Al Cheit* (lit., 'For the sin . . .') which, with its introduction (here omitted) is called *Vidui Rabba*, 'The Long Confession.' It is found in the liturgy for Yom Kippur, and its use here is an innovation. It is first cited in the *Sheiltot*, a collection of discourses on the Pentateuchal lessons by Achai (c. 680-760), section 167, and SRA, p. 161. SRA has at most thirty verses (the manuscripts differ). In the

No. Page

Middle Ages it was greatly elaborated and arranged alpha-
betically. The Birnbaum High Holy Day PB has forty-four
(i.e., a double alphabetical acrostic); UPB II has ten; GOR
has eighteen; and *Gates of Repentance* has twelve (but
offers a number of differing selections in various services,
thus utilizing more of the trad. verses). Both UPB II (pp.
149f.) and GOR (pp. 159f.) offer *thematic*, not alphabetical,
arrangements. *Gates of Repentance* follows their example
(See, e.g., pp. 271f., from which the present selection is
largely taken).

73 43 *For all these* . . . The concluding paragraph of *Al Cheit* (See
        above).

74 43 *We have sinned against life* . . . A free adaptation by CS of
        an unpublished reading by JR on the theme of *Al Cheit* (See
        No. 73). Following a suggestion by Rabbi Robert I. Kahn,
        CS has included the opening Hebrew words of Al Cheit.
        First used in *Gates of Repentance*, p. 404.

75 44 *For all these* . . . See No. 73.

76 45 *God before whom* . . . New, by CS, based on a meditation
        by John Baillie. The penultimate sentence is Ps. 51.12, slight-
        ly adapted by a change from 1st person singular to 1st
        person plural. See *Gates of Repentance*, p. 405.

77 45 *Keep me, O God* . . . A prayer by the Chasidic master,
        Elimelech of Lizensk (Poland, 1717-1787), reprinted in
        Language of Faith, (ed. by Nahum N. Glatzer, Schocken
        Books, Inc., N.Y., 1947, expanded ed.), p. 317. Freely trsl.
        and adapted by CS. The adaptation includes a change from
        1st person plural to 1st person singular.

78 45 *Our Father, our King* . . . The last verse of the famous peni-
        tential litany, known from its opening Hebrew words as

No. Page

Avinu Malkeinu. The litany as a whole is generally attributed to R. Akiva (the great 2nd C. Pal. sage) on the basis of a story in the Talmud (B. Ta-anit 25b) that once, during a drought, he prayed successfully for rain, his words corresponding to the first and last verses of this litany. On the one hand, however, Akiva may have used an already-established formula; on the other hand, it is certain that many verses were added after his time.

79   46   Our God above . . . This is from the *Selichot* in the Sefardi Ritual for the Days of Awe. See *The Forms of Prayer . . . of the Spanish and Portuguese Jews*, ed. by Isaac Leeser, Phila., 1853, pp. 17ff. Trsl., abridged, and rearranged by CS. The similarity of this litany to *Avinu Malkeinu* (See preceding Note) is evident.

80   47   We pray for compassion . . . Found in the *Tachanun* (penitential prayers) for the weekday service, and in the trad. *Selichot*. The second verse is the last verse of *Avinu Malkeinu* (See No. 78). It is given, almost as here, in SRA, p. 160 (in the RH liturgy).

81   47   Uncertain of our ways . . . An arrangement of Scriptural verses, attributed by Rosenfeld, p. 22, to a liturgical poet named Amitai (Italy, 780-850). The quotations are: II Chron. 20.12; Pss. 25.6; 33.22; 79.8; 123.4; Habbakuk 3.2; Pss. 103.14; 79.9. It is found in the *Tachanun* (See No. 80) and in the trad. *Selichot*. SRA, p. 38, has all these verses, and two others as well. MV, p. 71, has them all, but in a slightly different order: the last verse here is there the first, and other verses are there included.

82   48   Help us to return . . . Lam. 5.21.

83   48   Tekiah Gedolah . . . The sounding of the Shofar here is an innovation, although, among Ashkenazi Jews, the Shofar is

No. Page

trad. sounded (in addition, of course, to the sounding on RH morning and at the conclusion of Yom Kippur) each day (except for Shabbat) during Elul, the month preceding RH. The Shofar was anciently used as an alarm, to announce the Jubilee year, and for other purposes; in some communities today it heralds the advent of Shabbat. Other uses (e.g., as part of the ceremony of excommunication) have fallen into desuetude along with their ancient occasions. In the Bible, the sounding of the Shofar is prescribed for all Festivals and New Moons (Num. 10.10), and especially on RH (Num. 29.10). Apart from announcing the advent of this season, the sounding of the Shofar at this time serves as a call to *Teshuvah,* 'turning,' and it is therefore appropriate for this service.

Acknowledgments

Every effort has been made to ascertain the owners of copyrights for selections used in this volume, and to obtain permission to reprint copyrighted passages. For the use of passages indicated, the Central Conference of American Rabbis expresses its gratitude to those whose names appear below. The Conference will be pleased, in subsequent editions, to correct any inadvertent errors or omissions that may be pointed out.

FARRAR STRAUS & GIROUX: From *At the Turning,* by Martin Buber, copyright © 1952. Reprinted by permission.

HARPER & ROW, PUBLISHERS, INC.: From *Eclipse of God,* by Martin Buber, copyright © 1952; and from *The Art of Loving,* by Erich Fromm, copyright © 1974.

HOLT, RINEHART & WINSTON: 'Being a Jew,' by Aaron Zeitlin, in *A Treasury of Yiddish Poetry*, edited by Irving Howe and Eliezer Greenberg, copyright © 1972; and 'Acquainted With the Night,' by Robert Frost, in *The Poetry of Robert Frost*, copyright © 1928, 1956, and 1969.

HORIZON PRESS: From *The Origin and Meaning of Hasidism* , by Martin Buber, copyright © 1960.

JEWISH PUBLICATION SOCIETY OF AMERICA: 'Psalm XXIV,' by A. M. Klein, in *Poems*, copyright © 1944. This material is copyrighted by and used through the courtesy of the Jewish Publication Society of America.

DENISE LEVERTOV: 'The Jacob's Ladder,' copyright © 1961 by Denise Levertov Goodman. Reprinted by permission of New Directions Publishing Corporation.

McGRAW-HILL BOOK CO.: 'Letter to the Front,' by Muriel Rukeyser, in *Collected Poems of Muriel Rukeyser*, copyright © 1978.

HOWARD NEMEROV: 'The View from Pisgah,' in *The Next Room of the Dream*, by Howard Nemerov, copyright © 1962. Reprinted by permission of the author.

PRAYER BOOK PRESS, INC.: From Jack Riemer, in *New Prayers for the High Holy Days*, copyright © 1970, 1971.

SCHOCKEN BOOKS, INC.: Ten excerpts from *The Essence of Judaism*, by Leo Baeck, Revised Edition, copyright © 1948; three excerpts from *Isreal and the World*, by Martin Buber, copyright © 1948; and two excerpts from *The Way of Response*, by Martin Buber, ed. Glatzer, copyright © 1966. All the above material is copyrighted by Schocken Books Inc., and reprinted by permission of Schocken Books Inc.

THOMAS Y. CROWELL, CO.: From *Poems From the Hebrew*, by Uri Zvi Greenberg, copyright © 1973.

LITURGY COMMITTEE

OF THE

CENTRAL CONFERENCE OF AMERICAN RABBIS

Lawrence A. Hoffman
Chairman

SIDNEY BROOKS	WILLIAM SAJOWITZ
A. STANLEY DREYFUS	CHAIM STERN
HIRSCHEL JAFFE	EDWARD TREISTER

JOSEPH B. GLASER, *ex-officio*
W. GUNTHER PLAUT, *ex-officio*
ELLIOT L. STEVENS, *ex-officio*
GEORGE WEINFLASH, *for the American Conference of Cantors*

◆ ◆

Chaim Stern,
Editor